INTRODUCTION

My name is Mark Rush and I've been drawing and painting since my youth. The illustrations in this coloring book are a collection of sketches I have done over the years. When I get a chance to sketch landscapes, architecture, or just an interesting scene from my travels, I draw in pencil then later fill it in with pen and ink. Many of my compositions I'll do paintings from. I've found that using colored pencils to record the colors is very satisfying and consequently I came up with this book which is a compilation of sketches done over the years. There are many different adult coloring books on the market for flowers, geometric designs, etcetera, but this book offers a unique set of drawings that hopefully stimulates your mind and puts you in another place for a period of time.

Hopefully you enjoy my compositions and find time to create your own color schemes to complete them or use the reference color sketches as a guide line. Colored pencils are lighter then paint and can be used in layers to increase intensity and hue. Brush tip markers or colored pens can also be used, but are less forgiving if you make a mistake. When coloring a sky you can use a light blue for a solid cloudless sky, or you can leave areas white indicating clouds. Yellow, orange and red can be used for dramatic sunsets or sunrises. Water can have shades of greens and blues and often reflect the color of the sky. So use your imagination. It's up to you. Vegetation can include yellows, greens, blues, browns and various flowers of multiple colors. Shading can provide nice effects keeping in mind where the sun or light source is. Rock layers and geological formations provide a multitude of colored layers and contrasts.

If you're an aspiring artist, hopefully these drawings give you an idea on what a good composition consists of and then you can follow up by sketching your own and use the same coloring techniques applied here to complete them. I find artwork to be very satisfying, and at the end of a stressful day the answer to achieving some peace of mind.

If interested in my work you can contact me at markrushart@gmail.com, or to view my online gallery at http://mark-rush.artistwebsites.com.

INDEX OF ILLUSTRATIONS

2

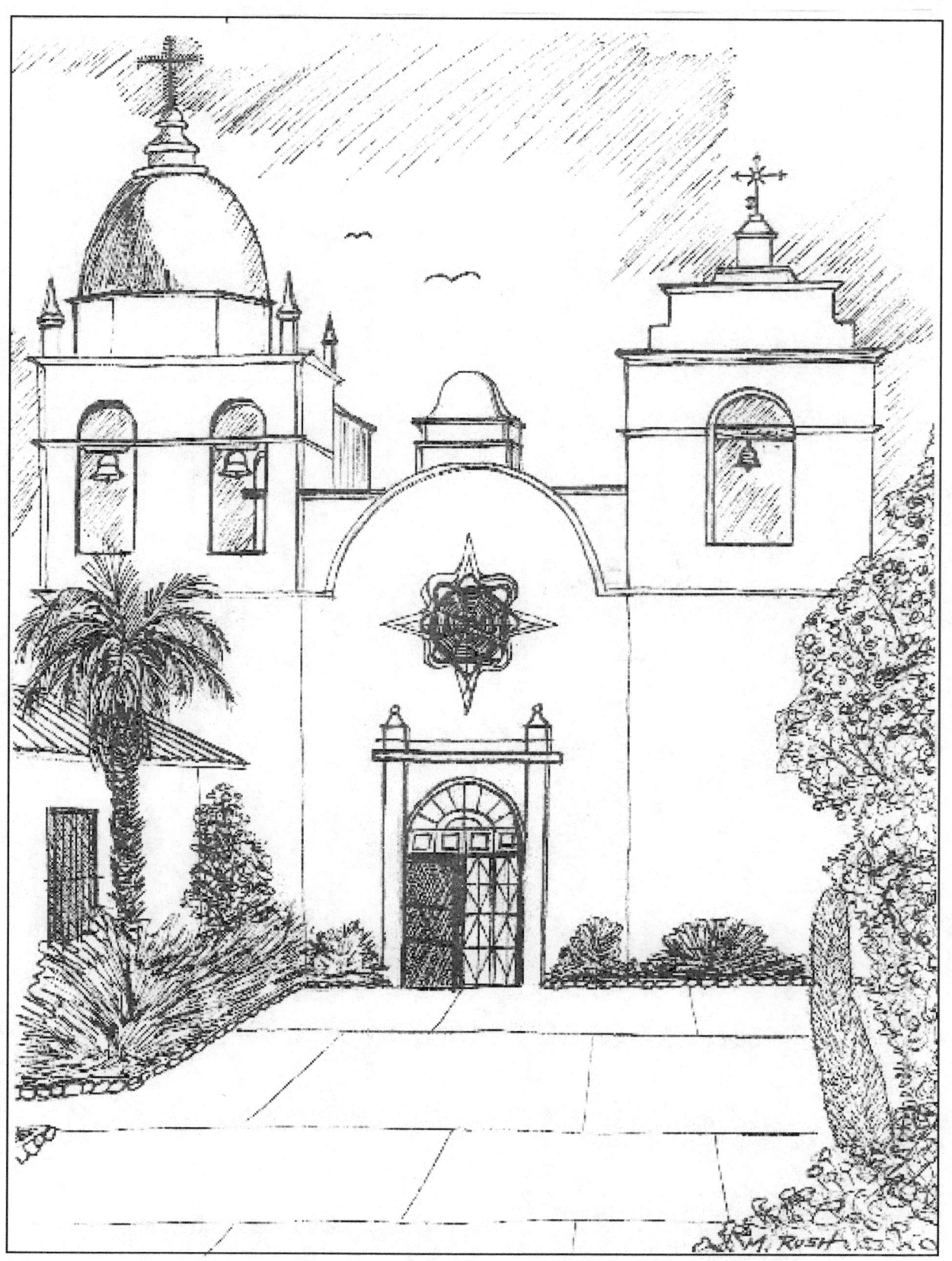

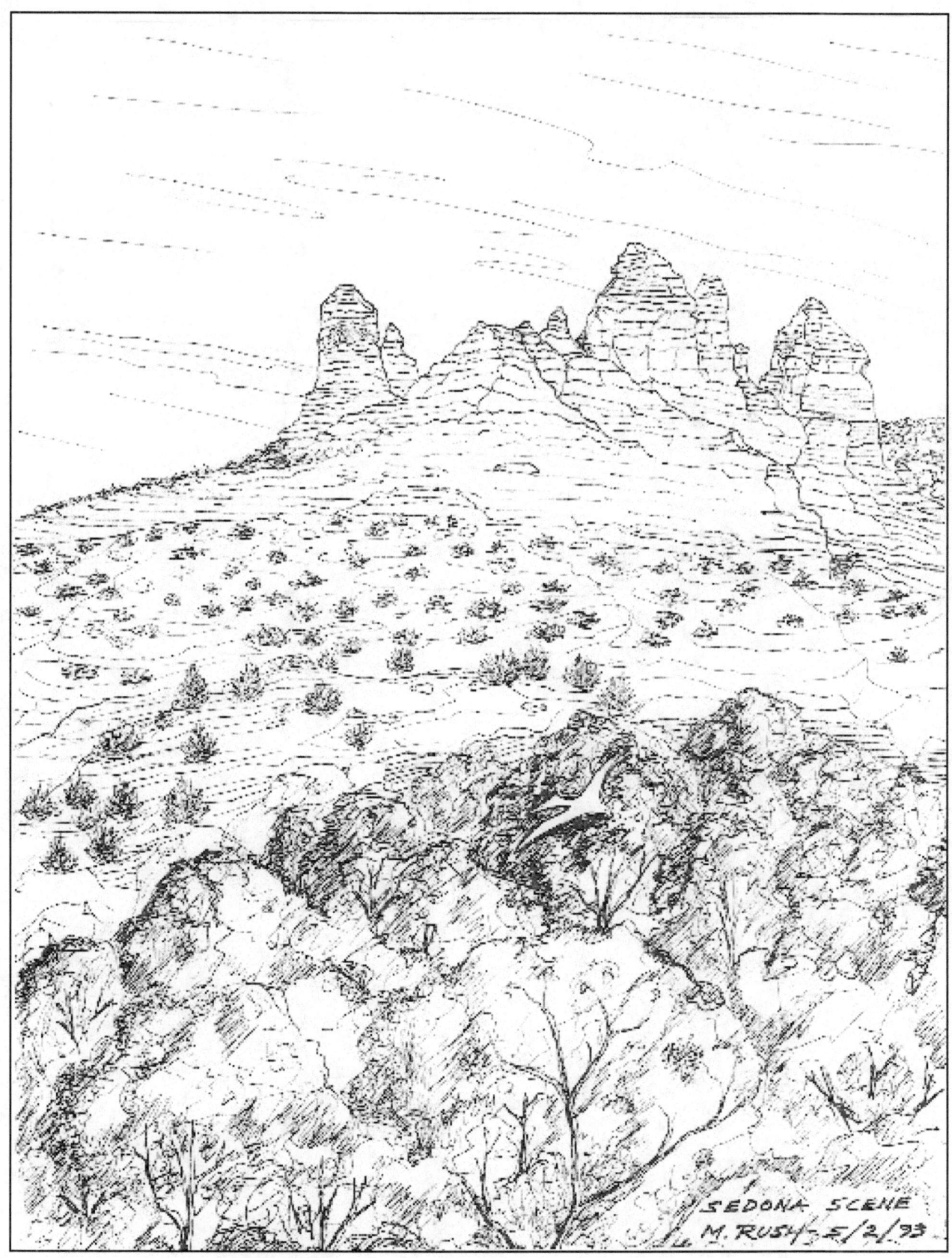

SEDONA SCENE
M. RUSH 5/2/93

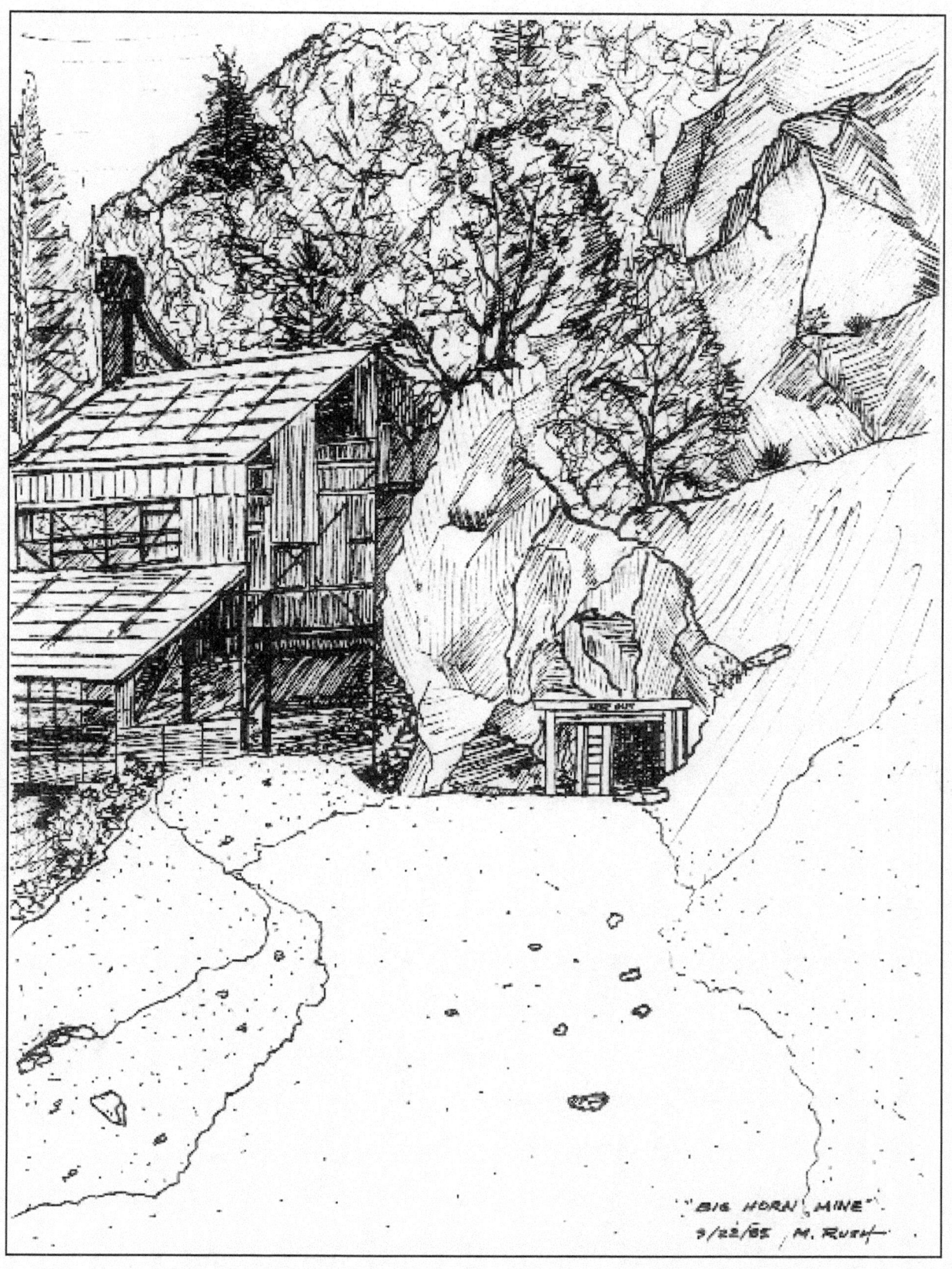

"BIG HORN MINE"
9/22/85, M. Rush

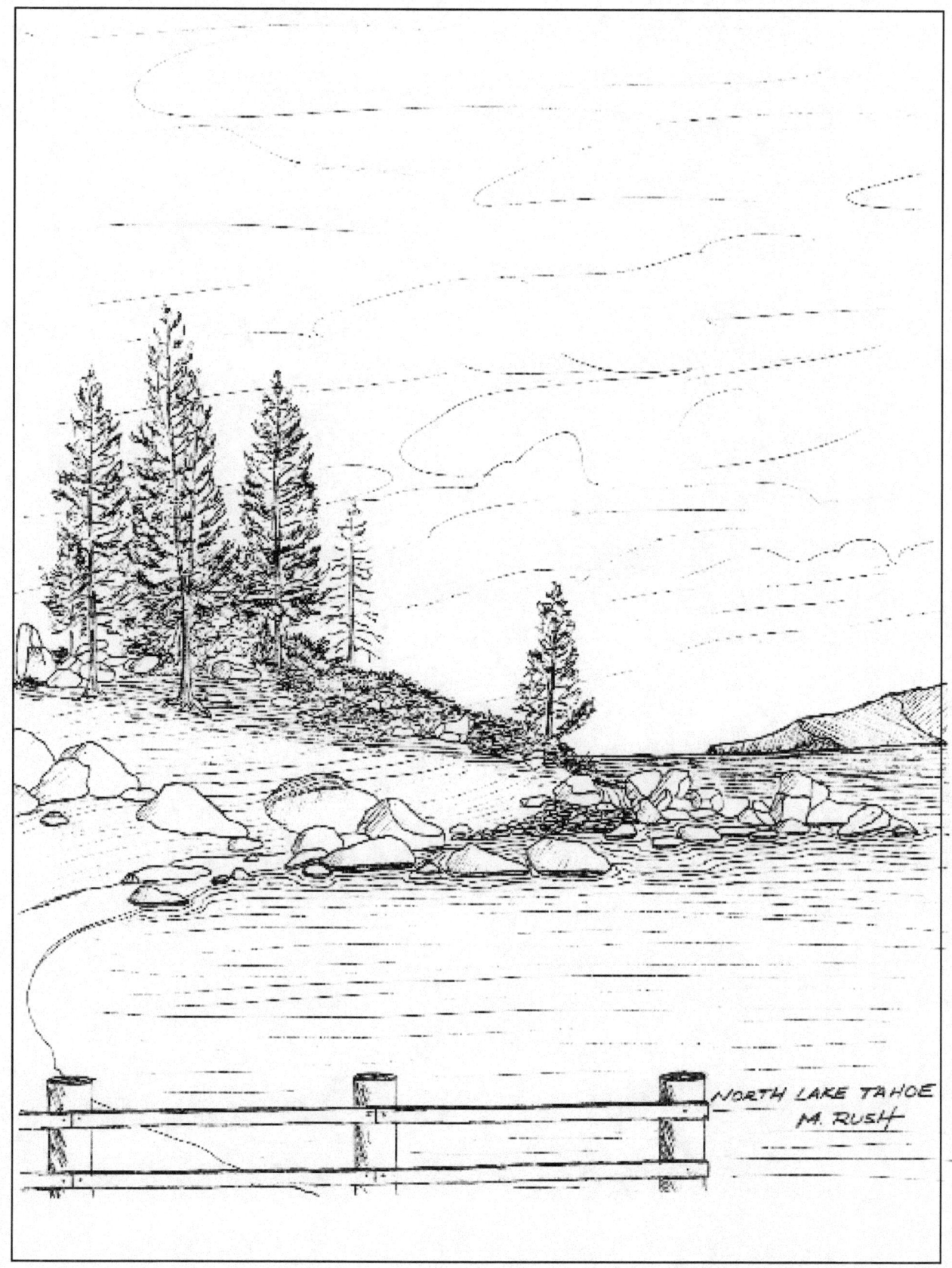

NORTH LAKE TAHOE
M. RUSH

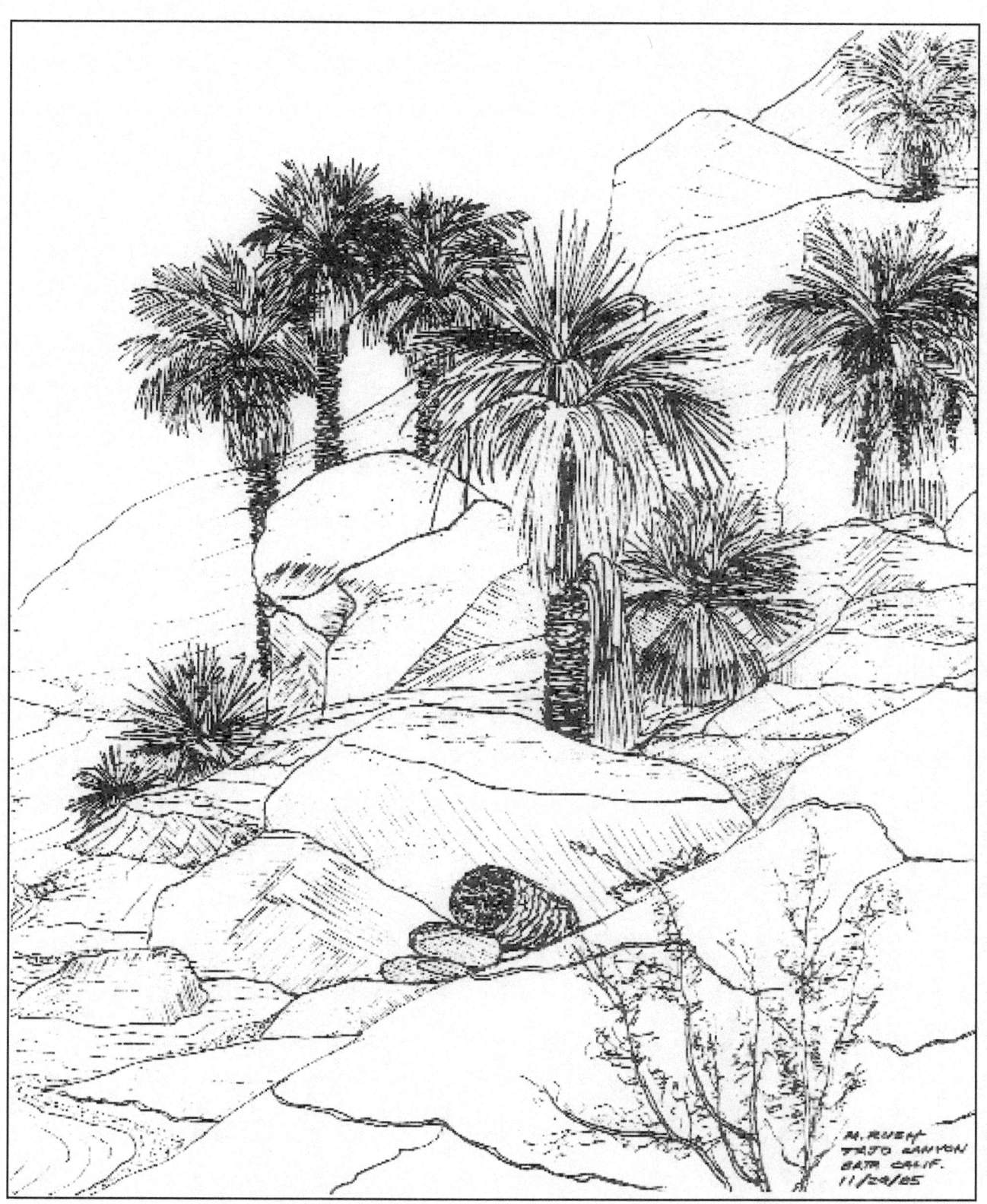

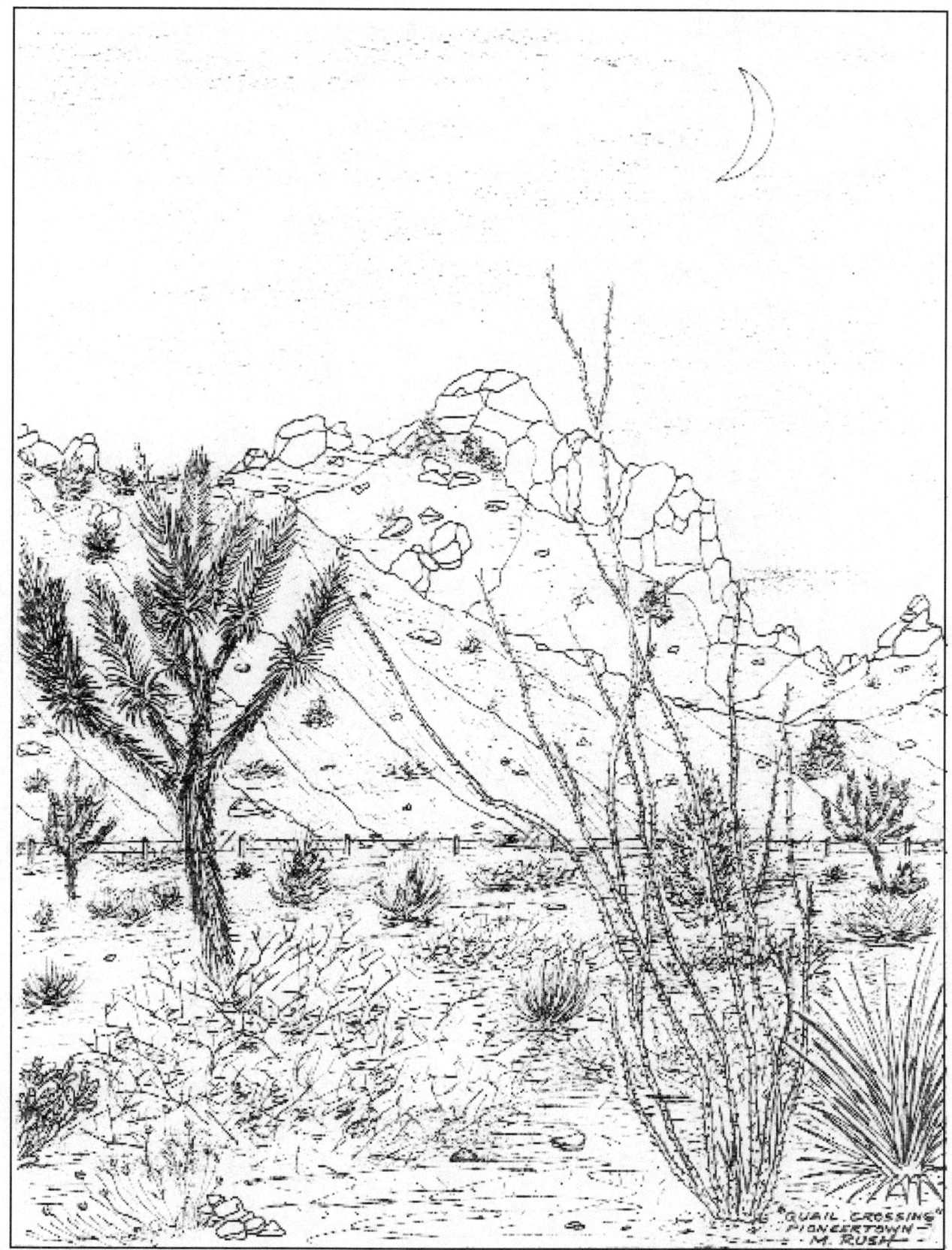

"QUAIL CROSSING"
PIONEERTOWN
M. RUSH

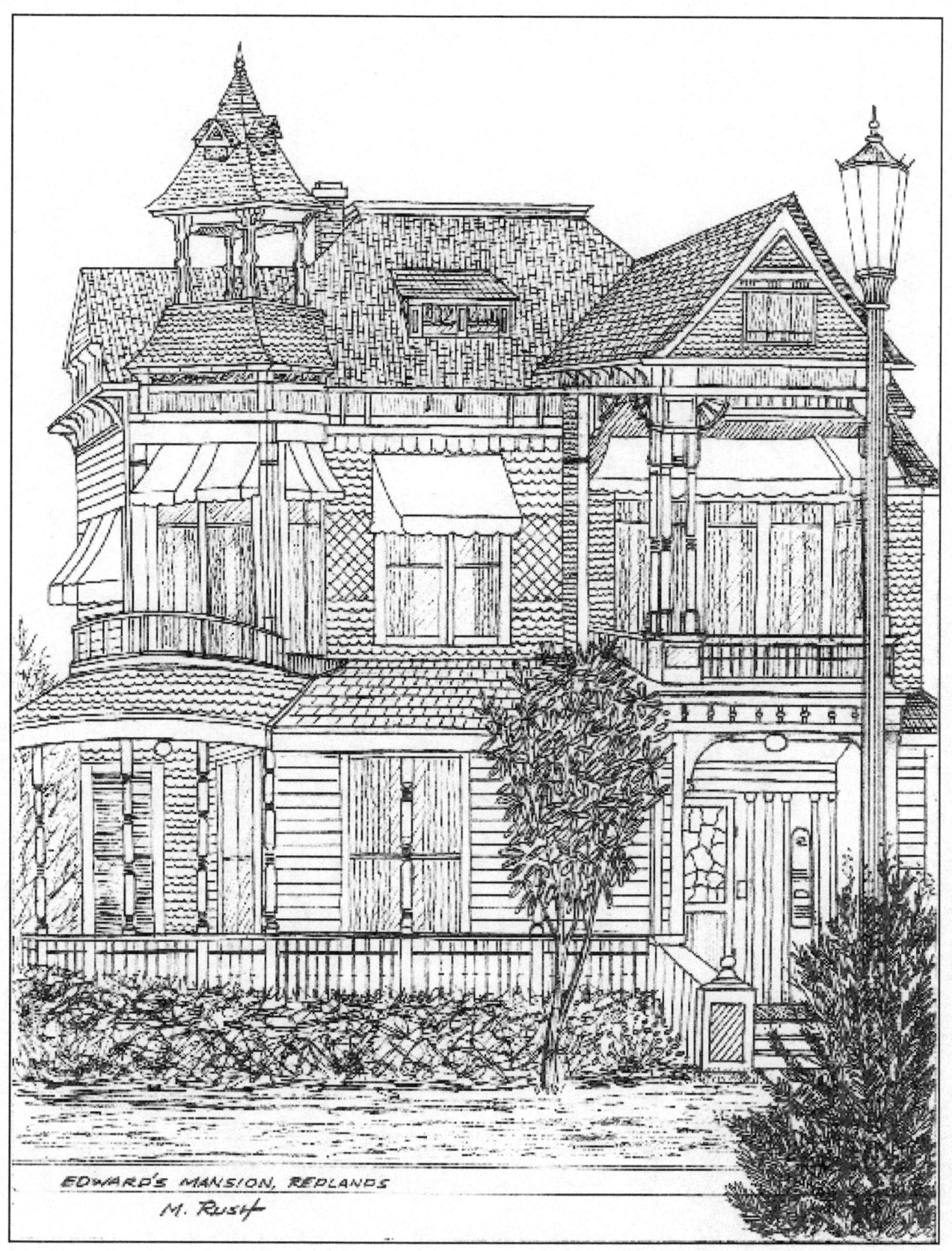

EDWARD'S MANSION, REDLANDS
M. Rush

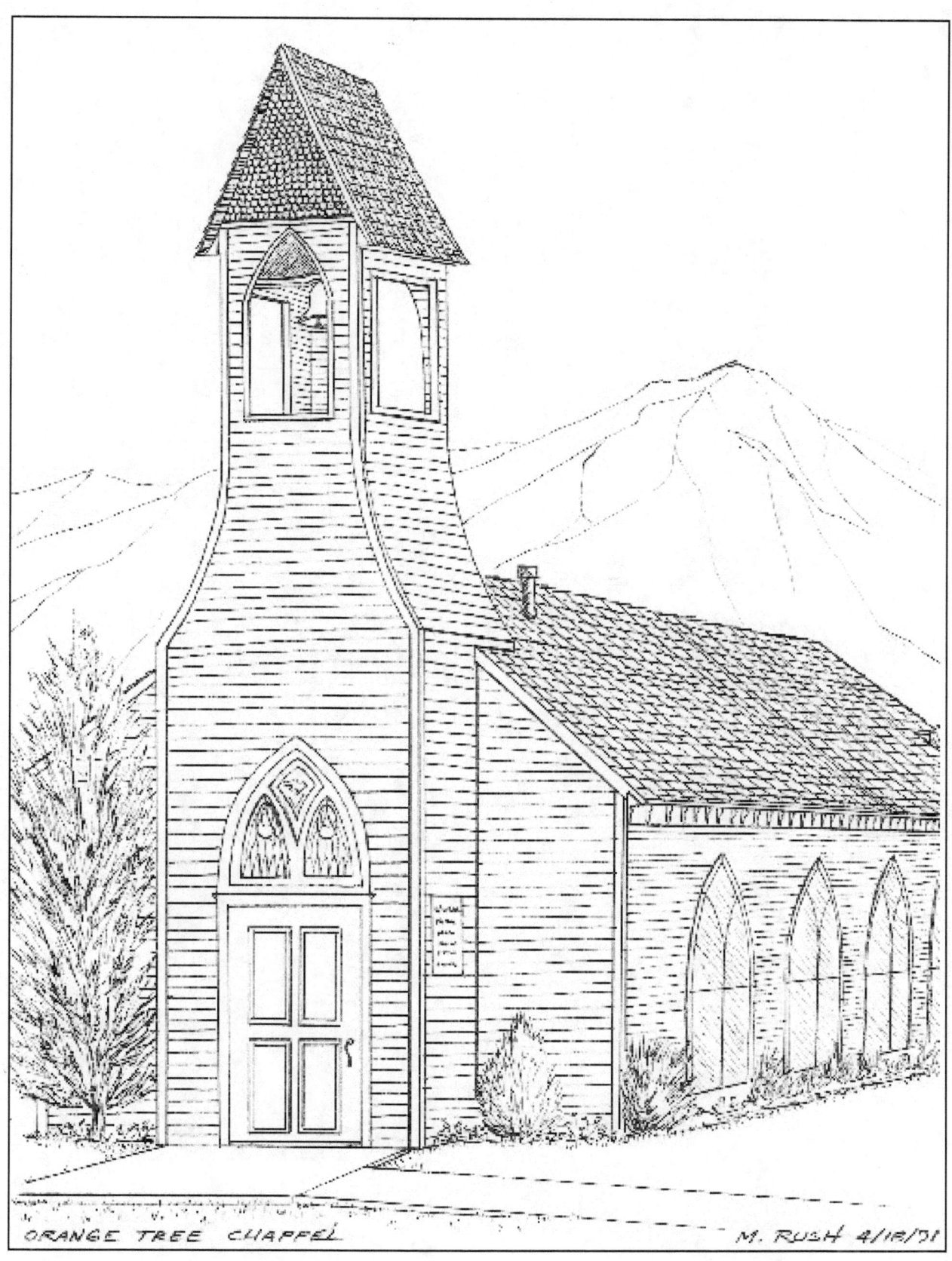

ORANGE TREE CHAPPEL   M. RUSH 4/18/91

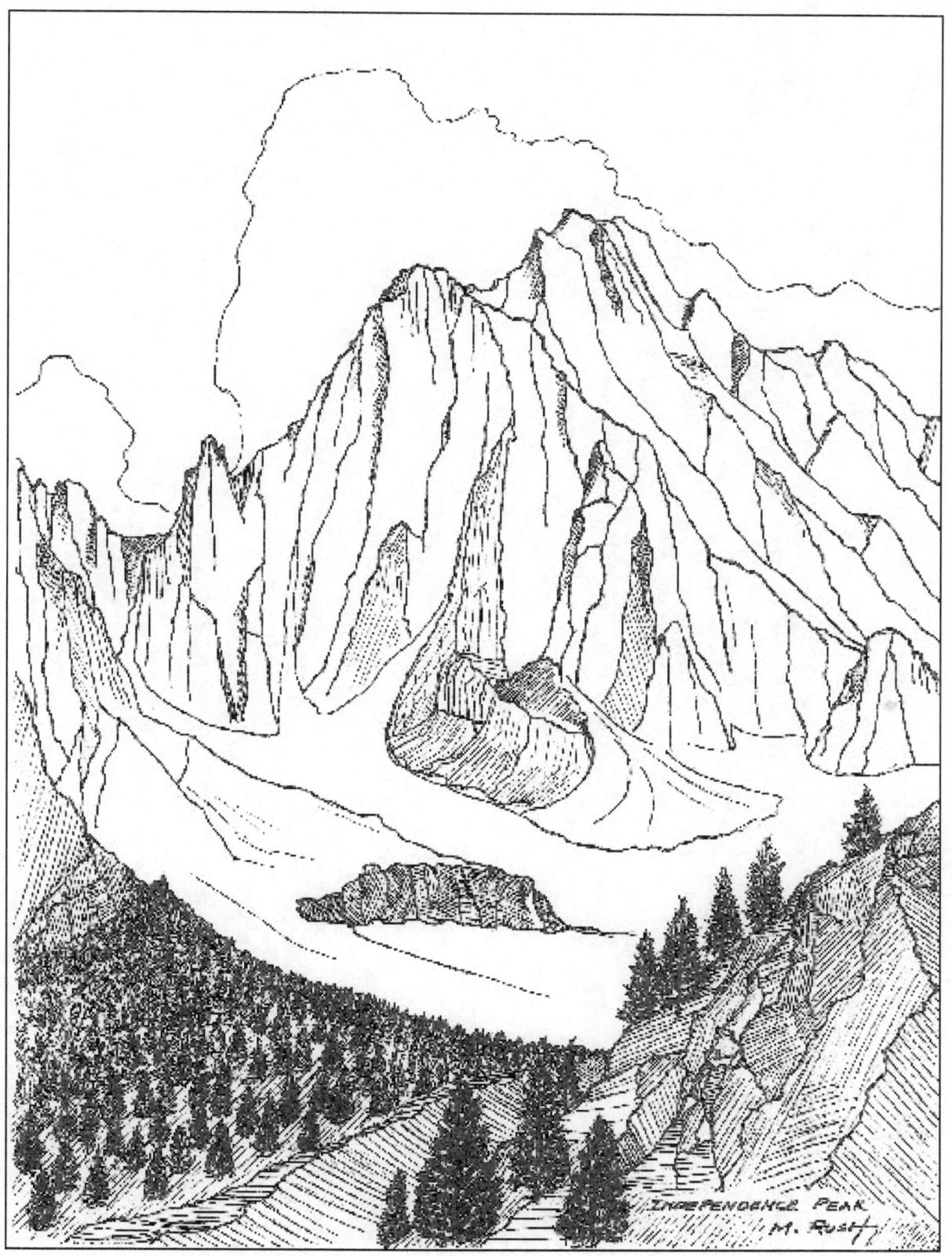

INDEPENDENCE PEAK

M. Rush

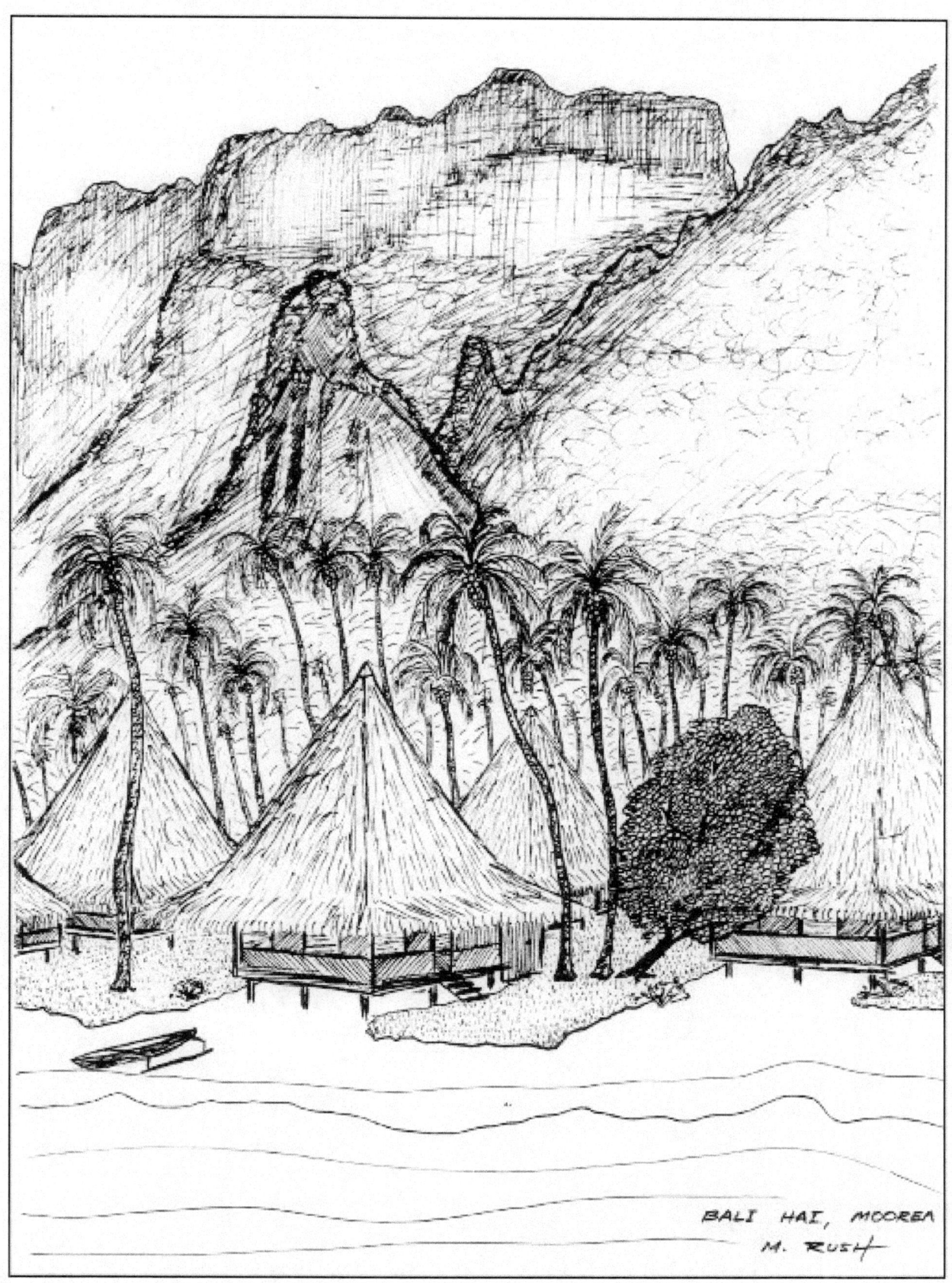

BALI HAI, MOOREA

M. RUSH

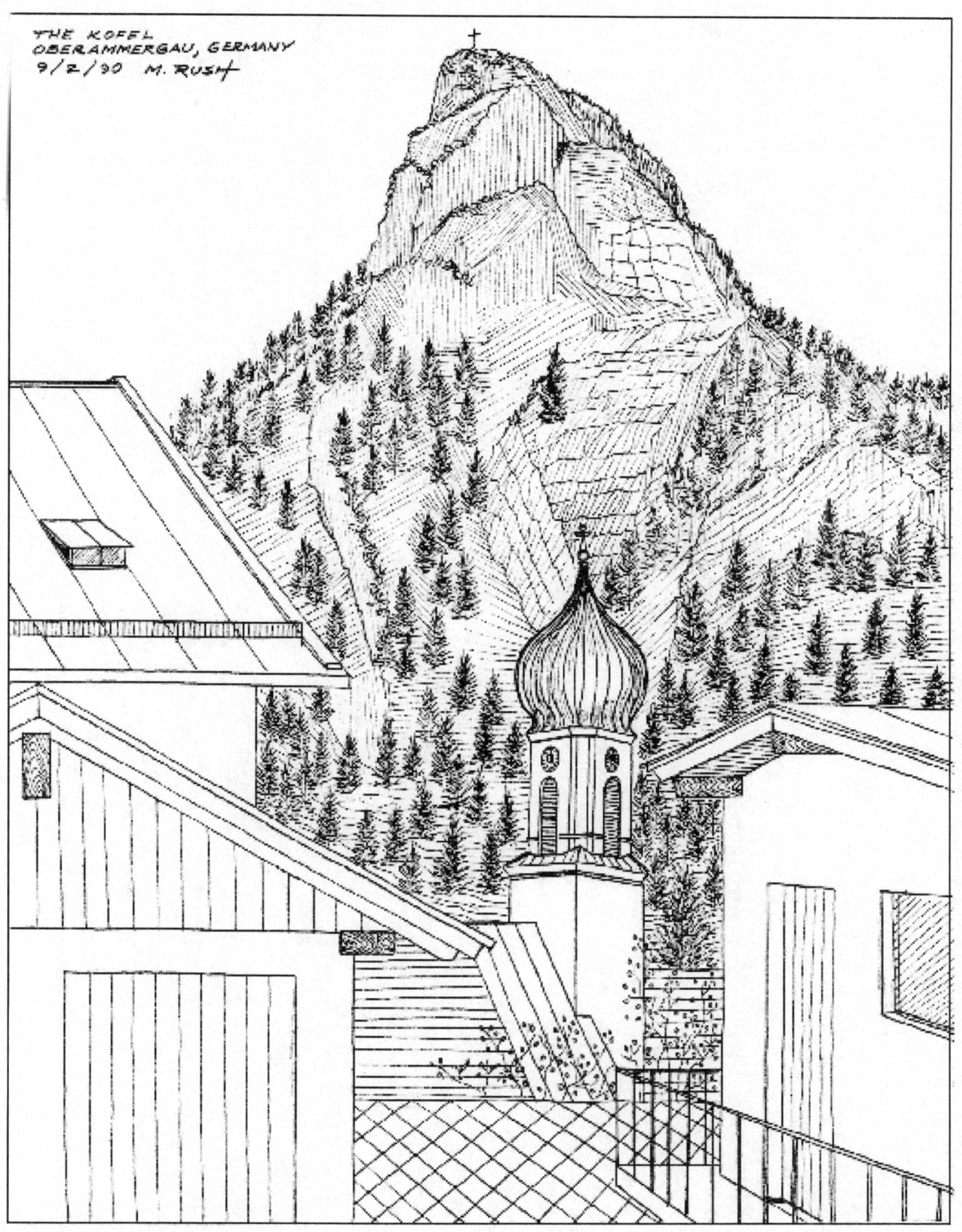

THE KOFEL
OBERAMMERGAU, GERMANY
9/2/90 M. RUSH

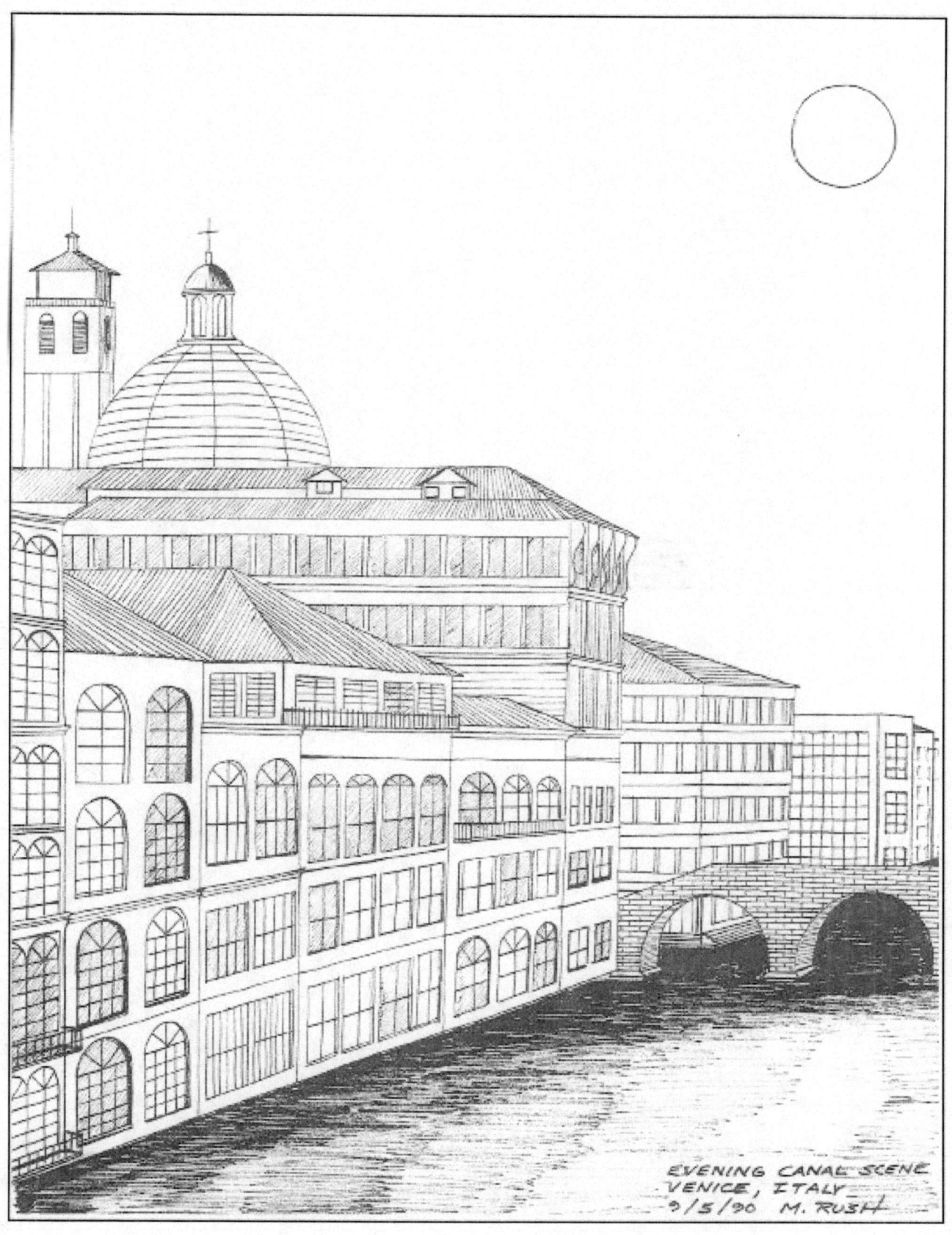

EVENING CANAL SCENE
VENICE, ITALY
9/5/90 M. RUSH

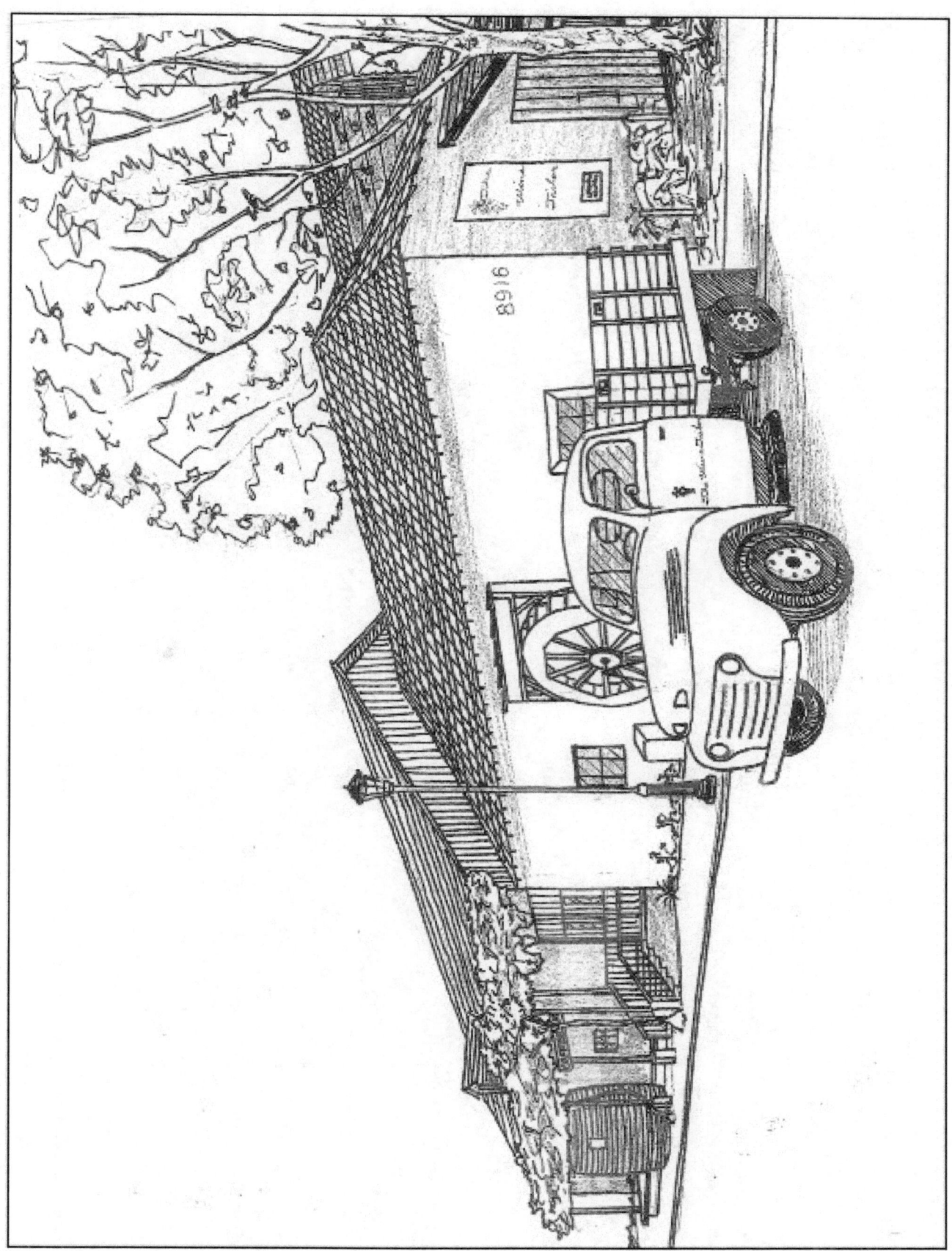

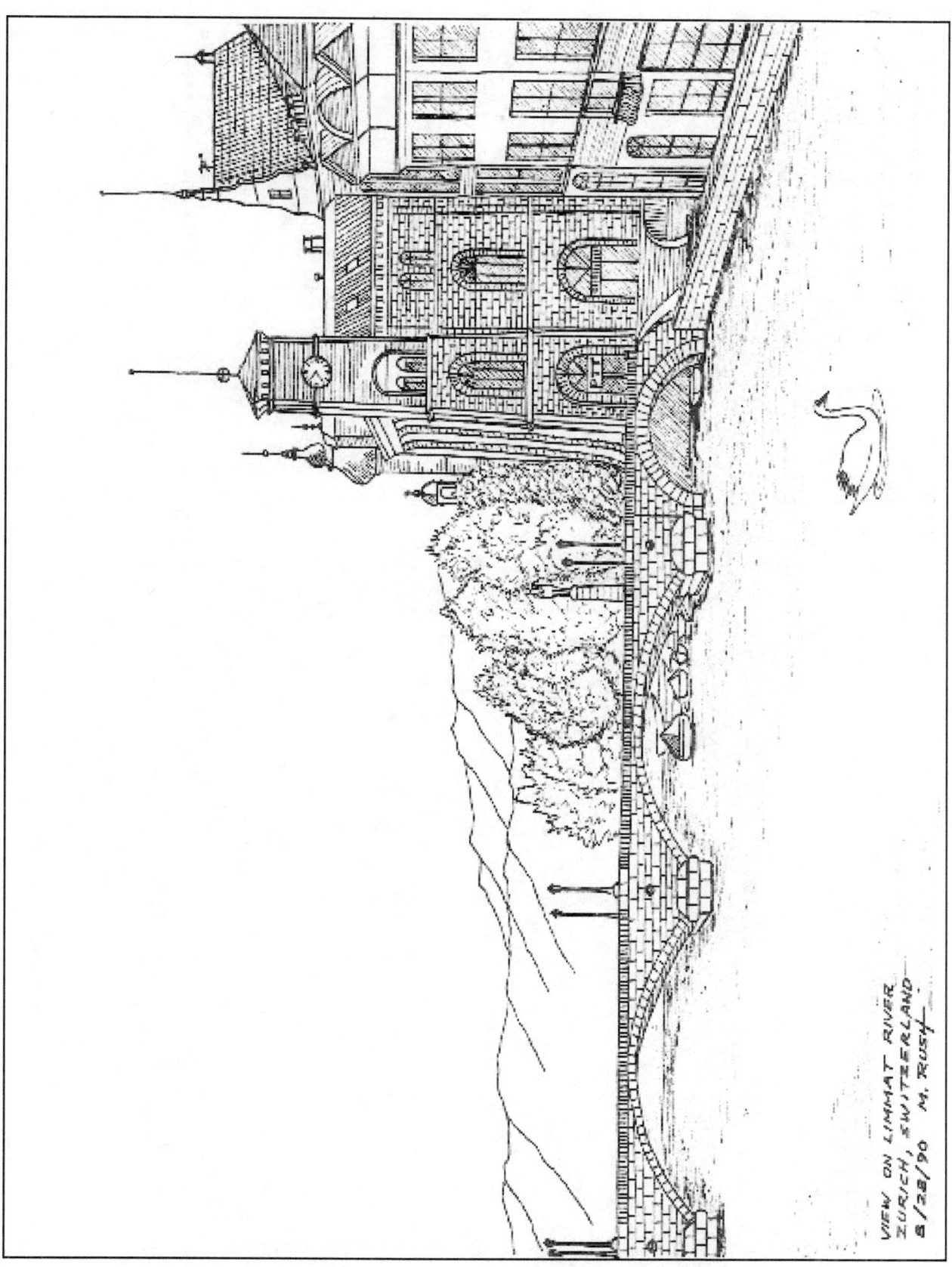

VIEW ON LIMMAT RIVER
ZURICH, SWITZERLAND
8/28/90 M. RUSH

29

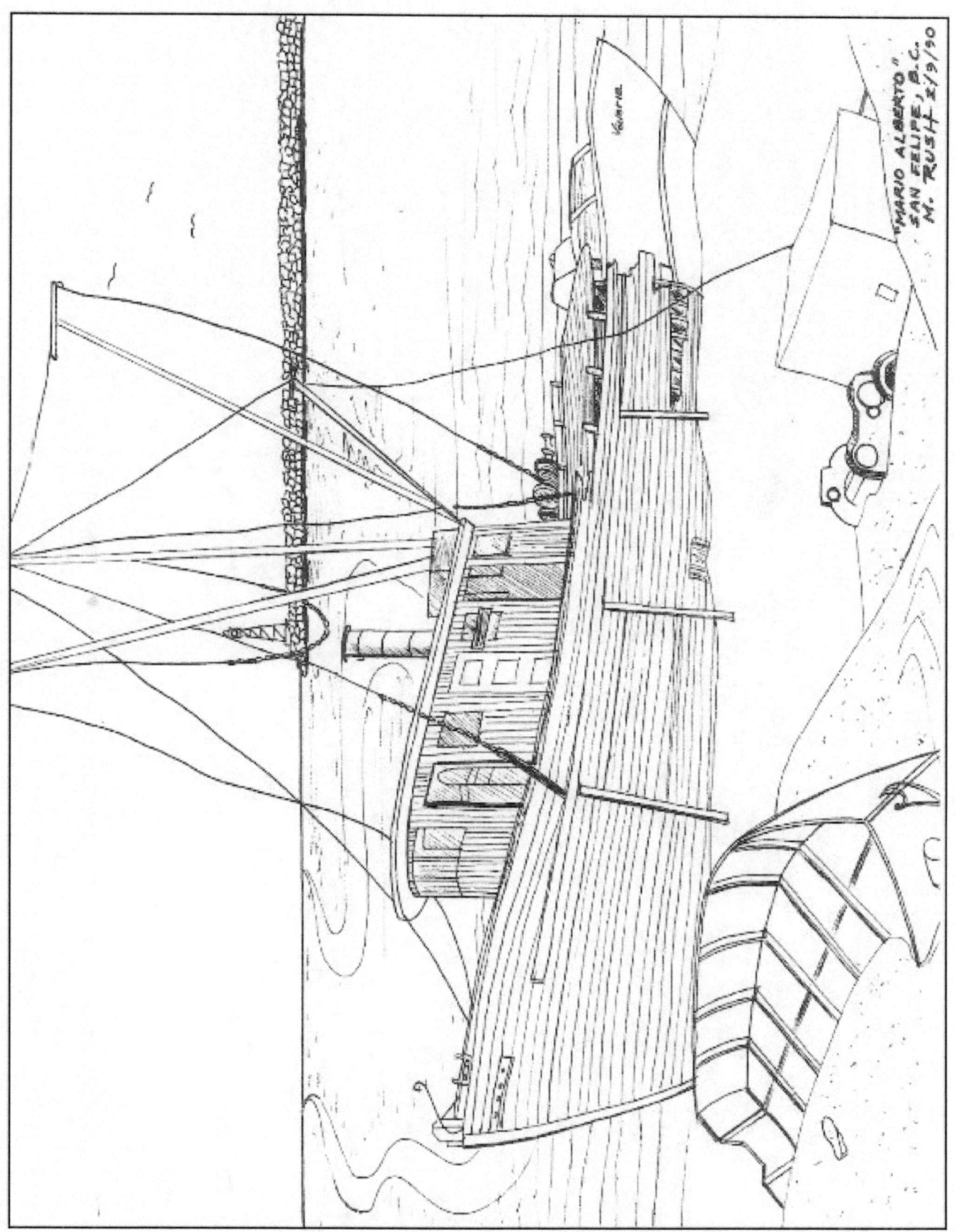

"MARIO ALBERTO"
SAN FELIPE, B.C.
M. RUSH 2/9/90

31

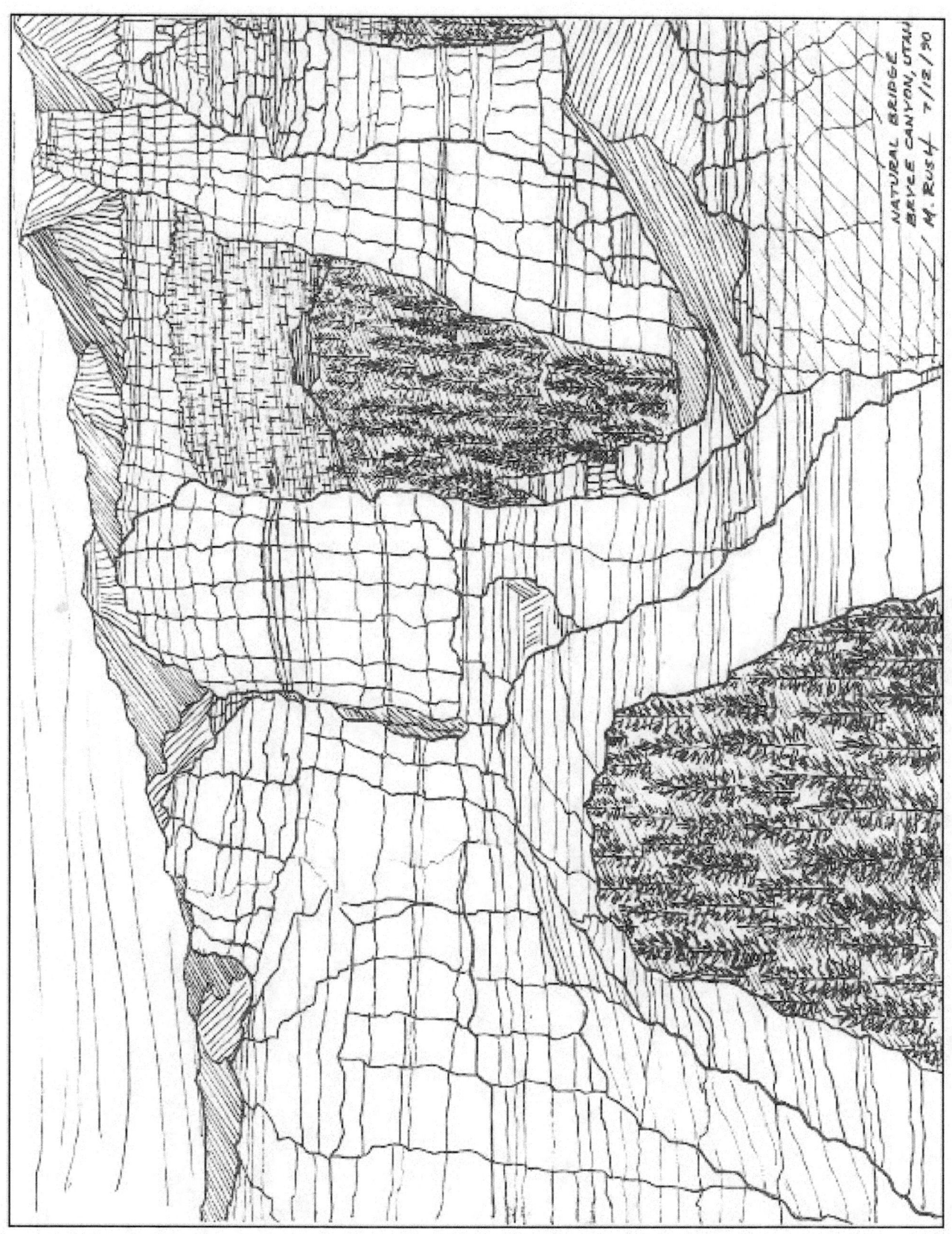

NATURAL BRIDGE.
BRYCE CANYON, UTAH
M. Rush 7/12/90

33

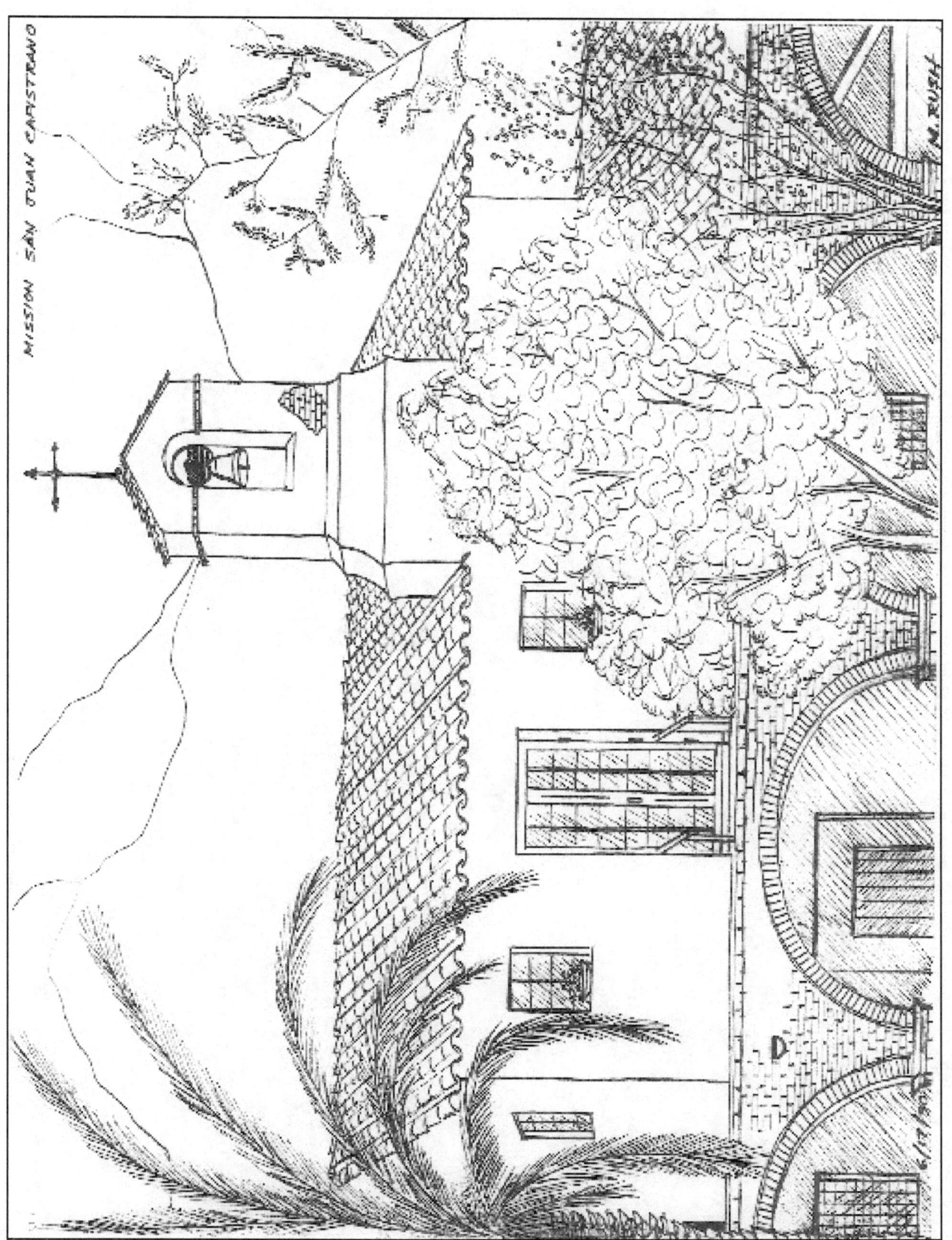

MISSION SAN JUAN CAPISTRANO

M. RUSH

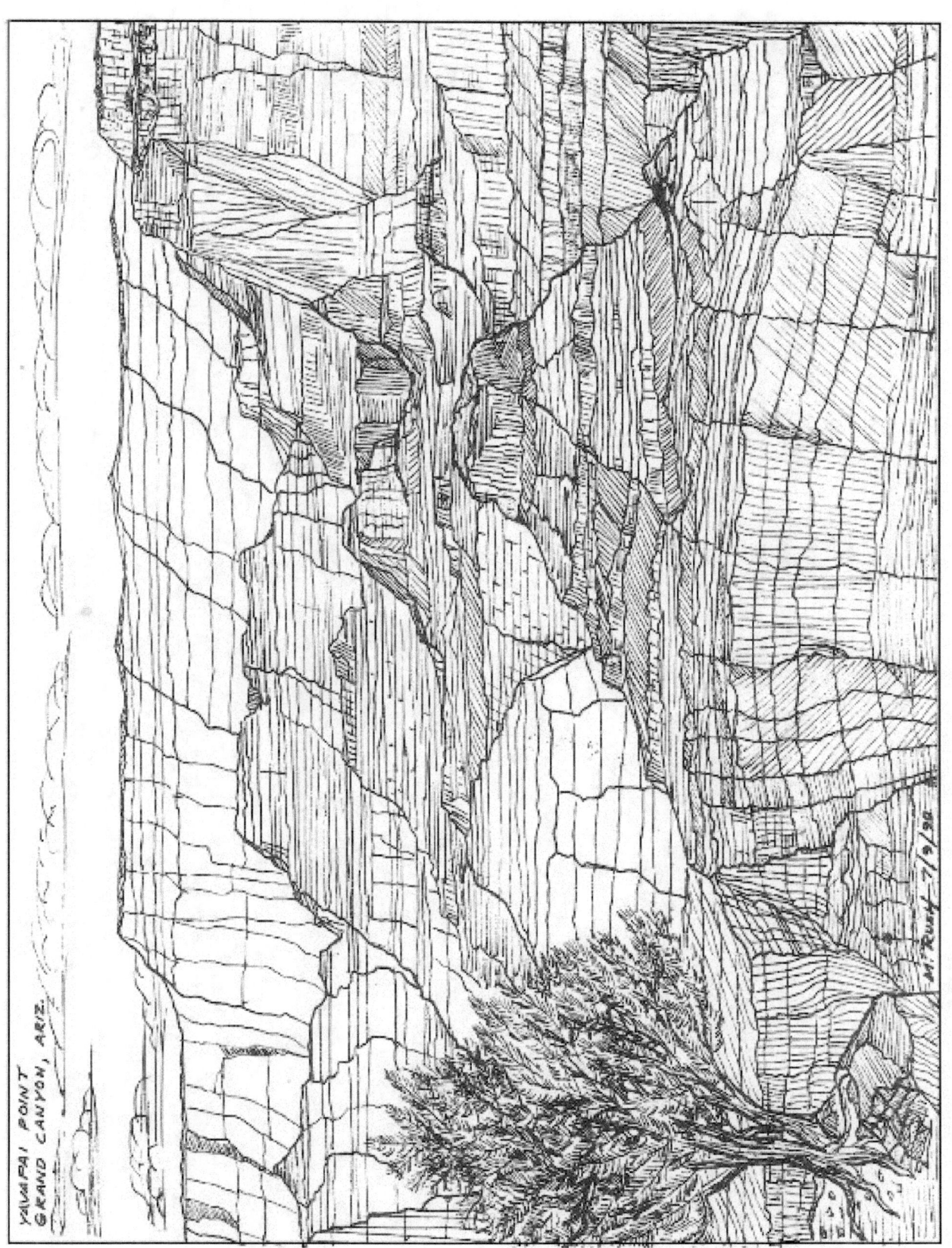

YAVAPAI POINT
GRAND CANYON, ARIZ.

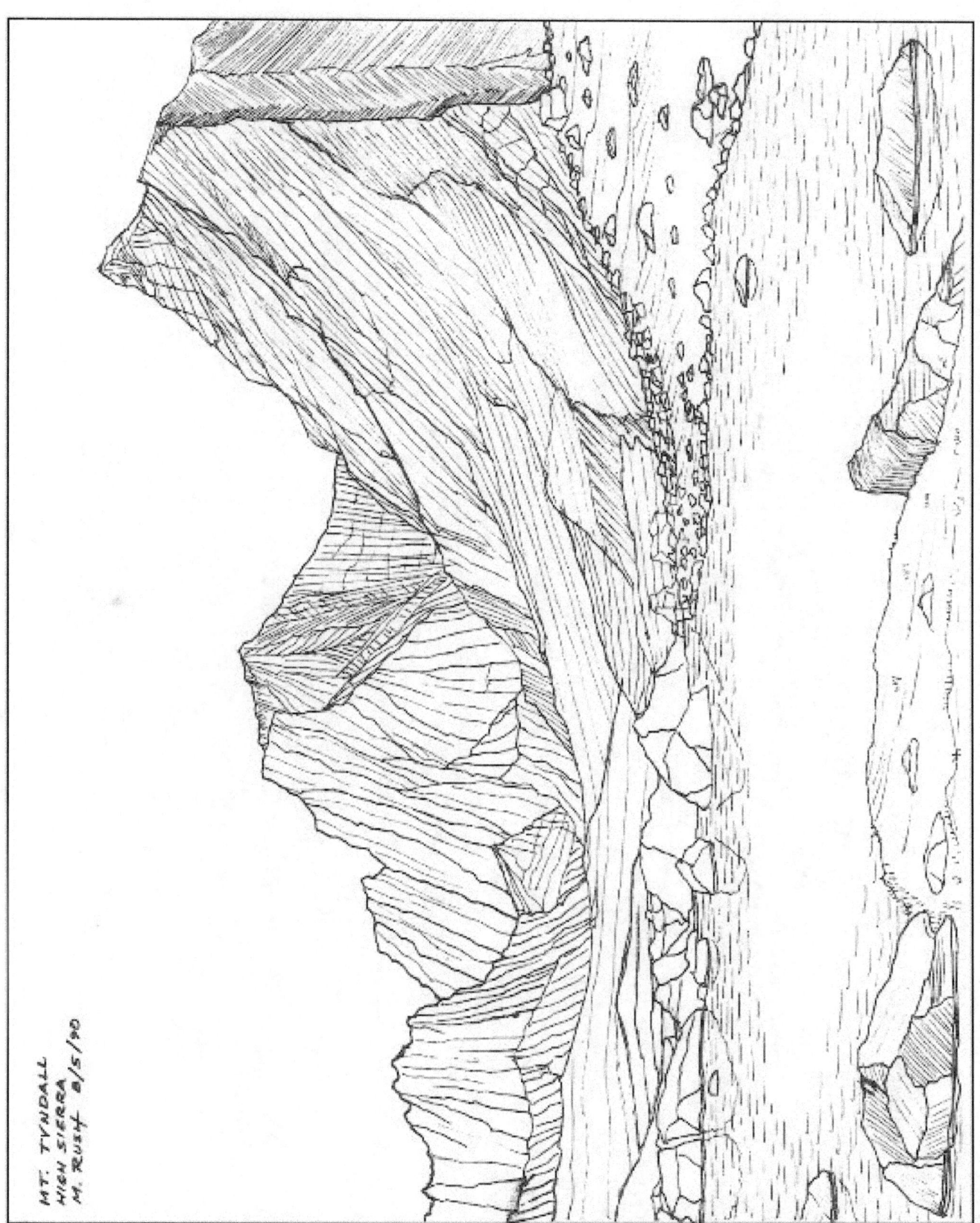

MT. TYNDALL
HIGH SIERRA
M. RUST 8/5/90

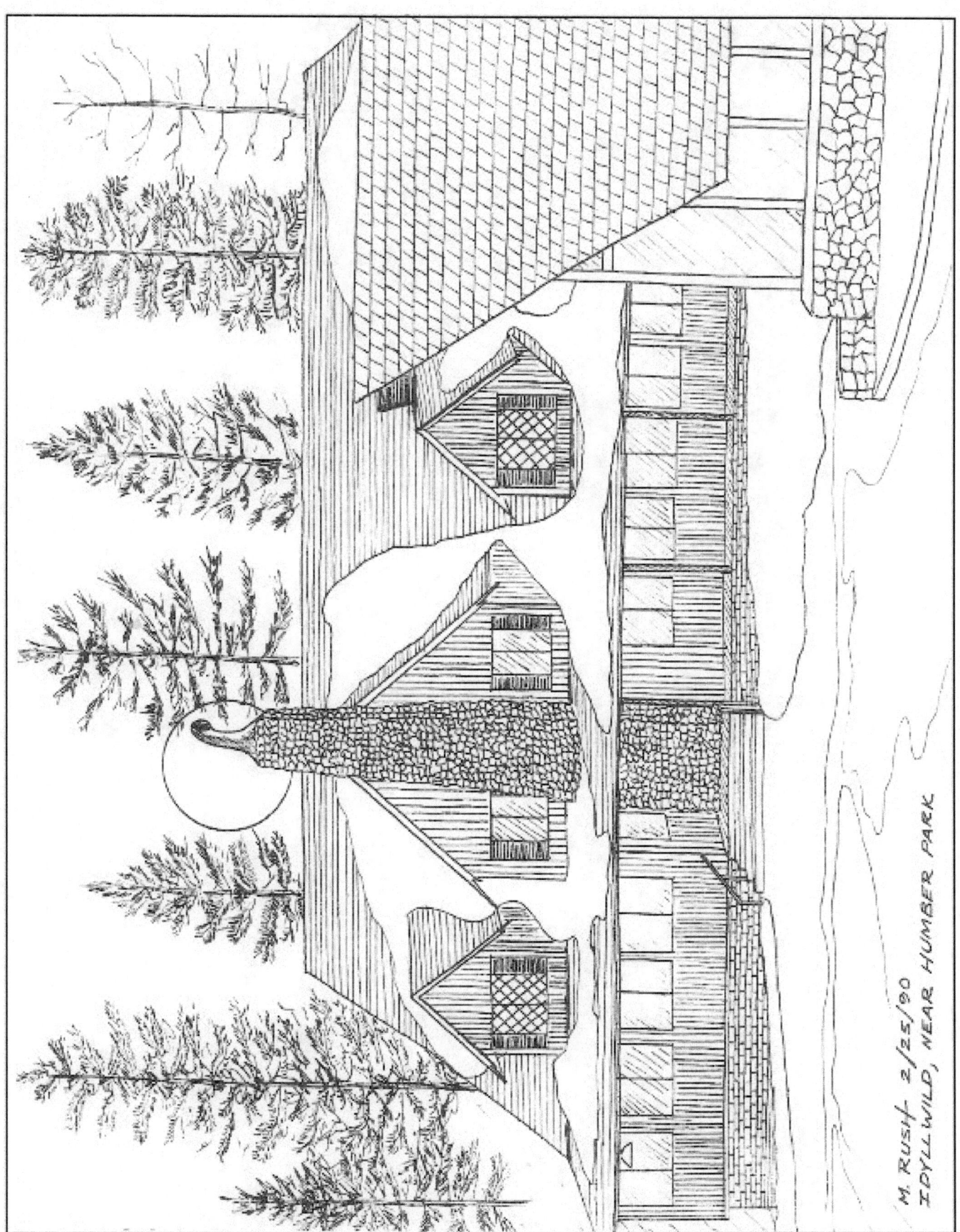

M. Rush 2/25/90
IDYLLWILD, NEAR HUMBER PARK

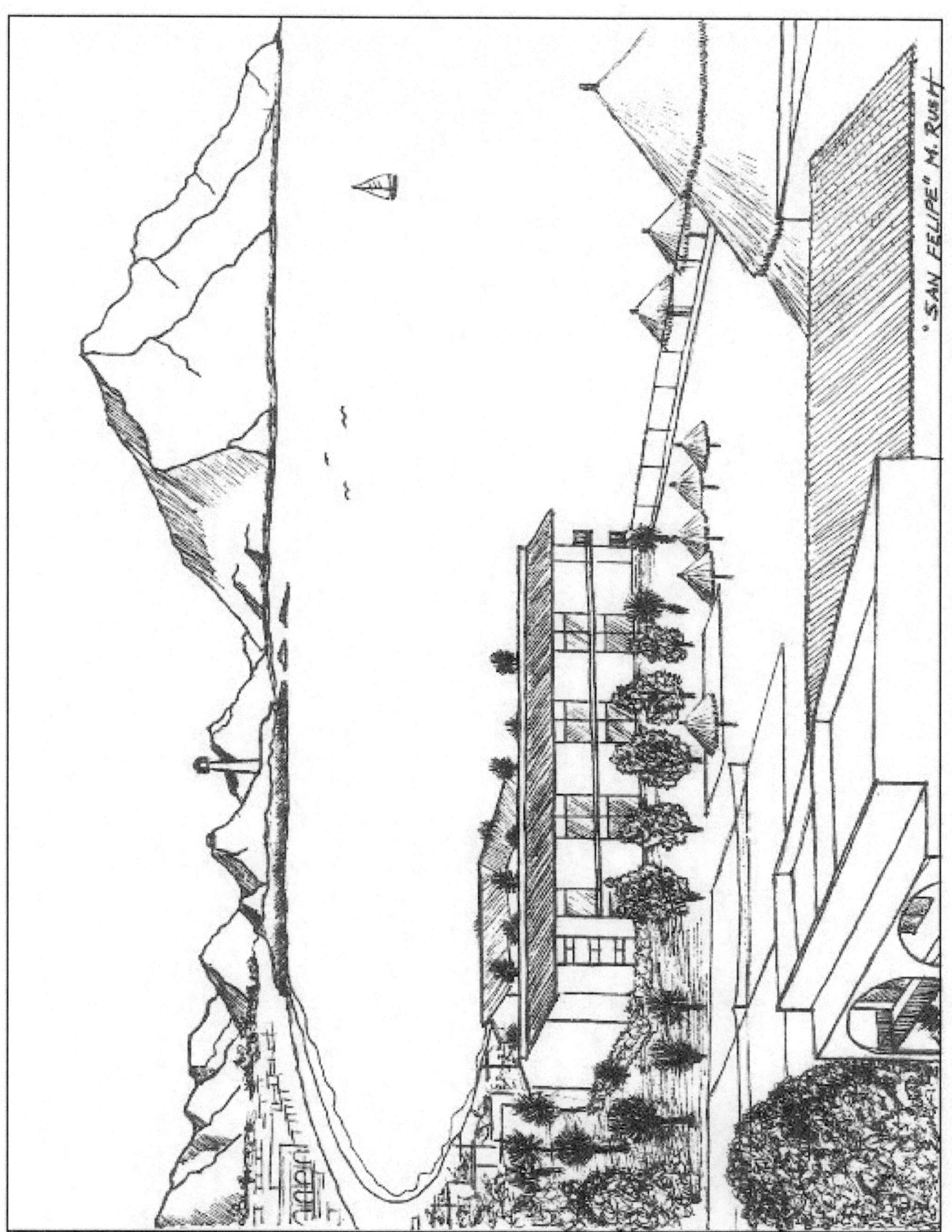

"SAN FELIPE" M. Rush

43

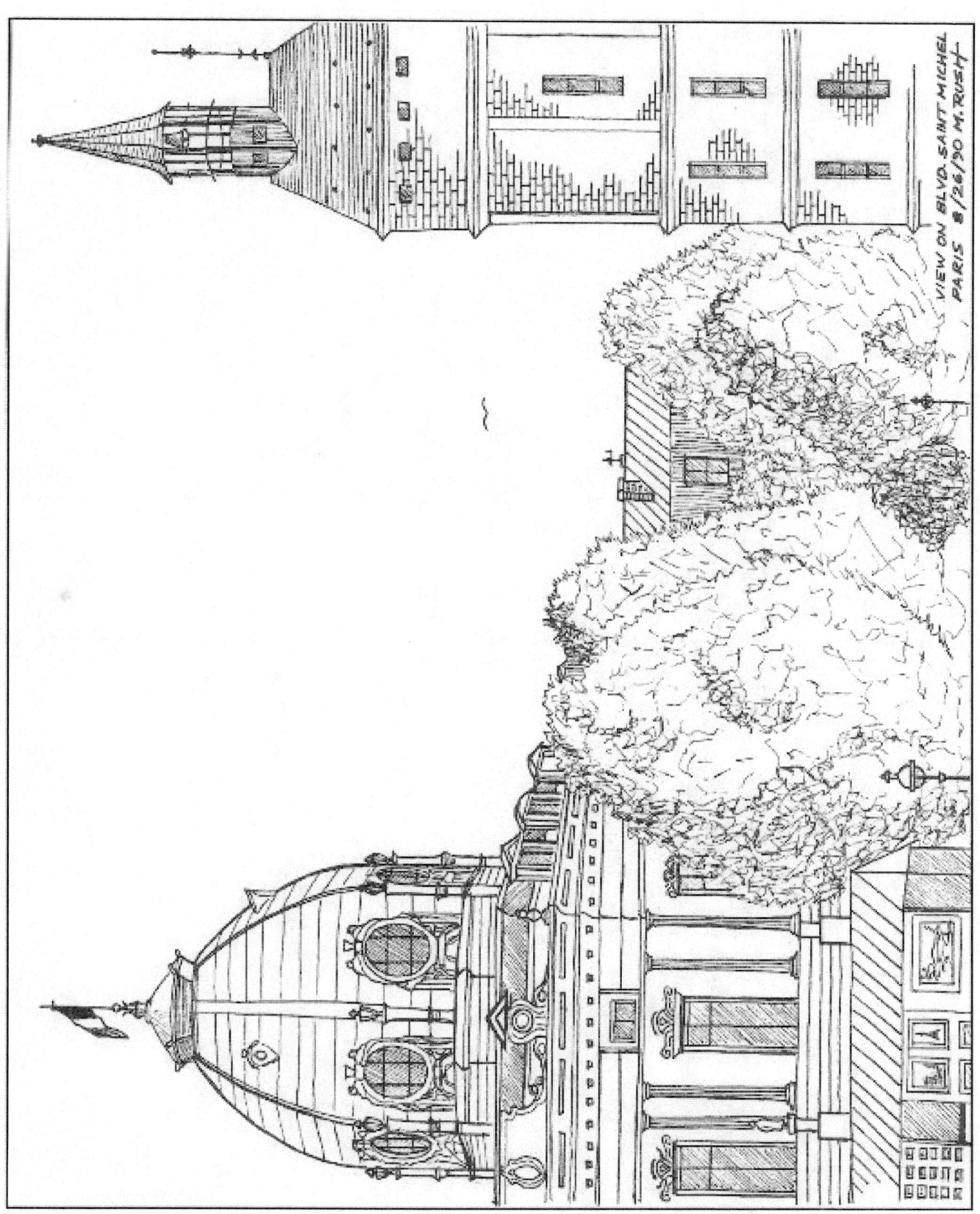

VIEW ON BLVD. SAINT MICHEL
PARIS 8/26/90 M. RUSH

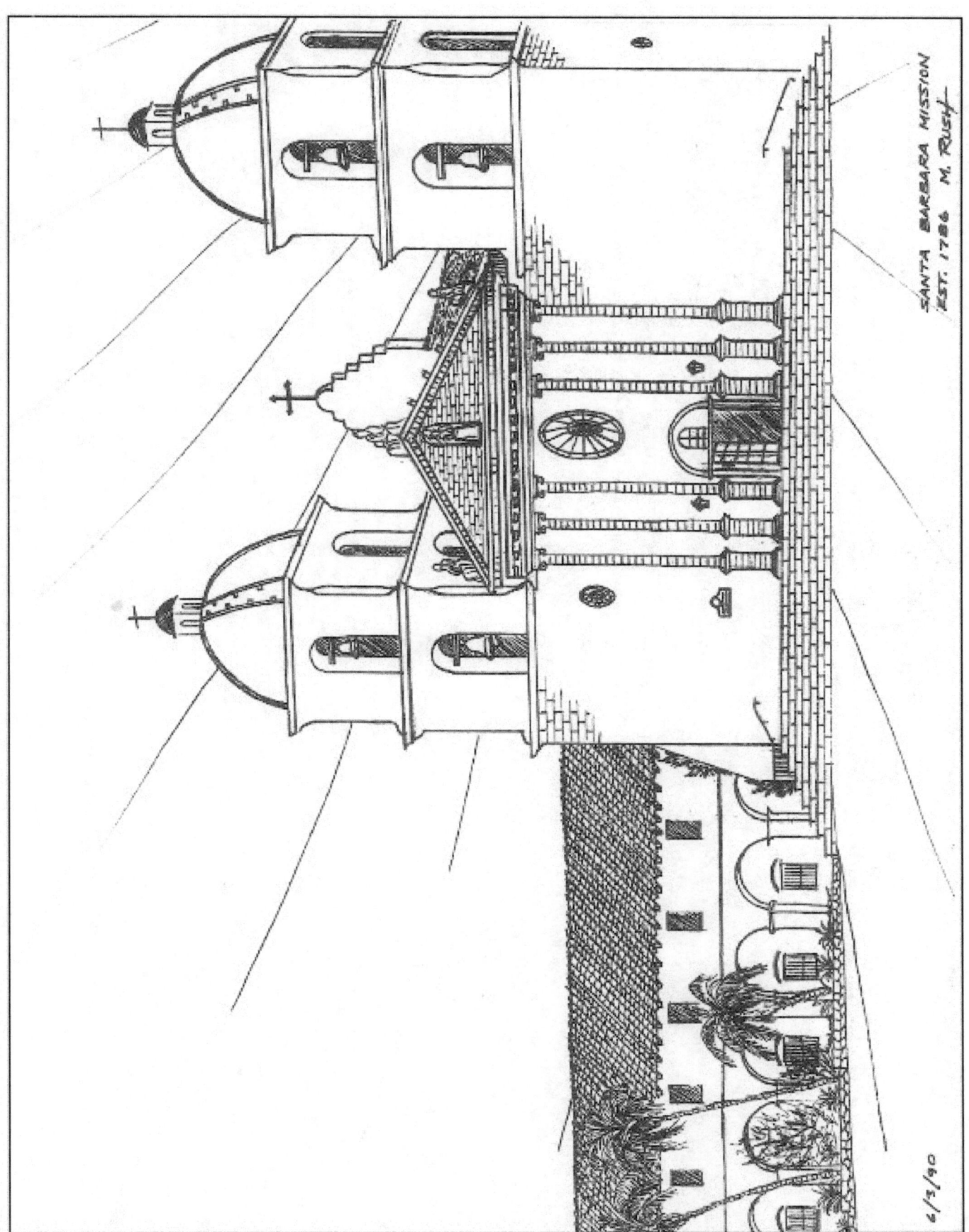

SANTA BARBARA MISSION
EST. 1786   M. RUSH

6/3/90

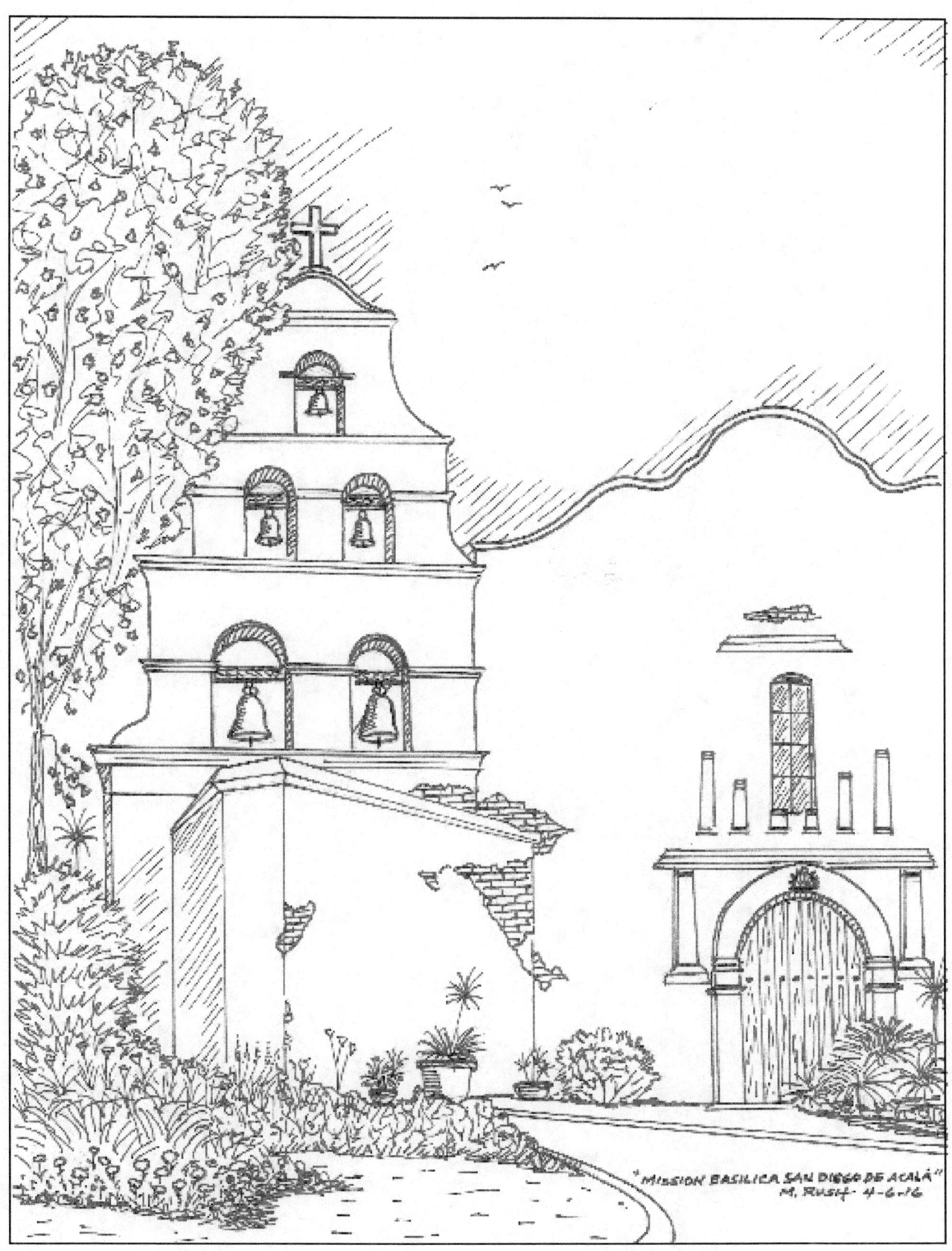

"MISSION BASILICA SAN DIEGO DE ACALÁ"
M. RUSH· 4-6-16